Yes,
It *is* All
About You

Yes, It *is* All About You

The ultimate guide for women:

putting yourself first,
getting what you've always wanted,
and feeling great at the same time

Dr. Jenna Eisenberg

Yes, It *is* All About You

Published by Iron Mountain Press
Wheaton, Illinois 60187

Copyright © 2007 by Jenna Eisenberg

Printed in the United States of America
Cover design by Life Success Publishing
Printing by Kjellberg Inc., Wheaton, Illinois

ISBN-10:   0-912868-11-2
ISBN-13: 970-0-912868-11-0

Dedicated to the love of my life, Ed

Acknowledgements
Thank you
for all the love and support and wisdom

Mary Bushman, Arlene Butler, Betty Anne Cyr,
Eva Dahm, Joshua Eisenberg, Carla Eisenberg,
Sheila Feigelson, Sharon Glass, Dawn Herbst,
James Malinchak, Sarge, Nirado Sloan,
Gillian Schneider, Ed Thomas,
and my patients: every single one of them.

To the memory of those whose life stories have inspired me.

CONTENTS

Author's Note

Dear Reader,

As a woman you were probably taught at an early age to take care of everyone and everything around you and to do it well. After marrying, raising children, starting a career, volunteering for hours at school or church, or any combination of these activities, there doesn't seem to be much left over for you.

It doesn't have to be this way. It's your life and <u>Yes, It *is* All About You</u>. Marianne Williamson says it beautifully in her book:

"Our deepest fear is not that we are inadequate. Our deepest fear is that we are powerful beyond measure. It is our light, not our darkness that most frightens us. We ask ourselves, who am I to be brilliant, gorgeous, talented, fabulous? Actually, who are you not to be?"

I'm pretty sure you've already read lots of books on related subjects, and yet here you are. You still feel like maybe there's something else that, if only you knew, would make all the difference. Well, this book might not tell you anything you haven't heard before. Ooh, that's bad news, huh? And just *knowing* the information in this book doesn't make much of a difference either. Ouch, that's bad news, too!

Then what *can* this book do for you? It can empower you to finally put yourself first. And it can remind you of what you already know that motivates you to take *action*. It may fill in a few places where you are stuck because information is missing. But most importantly, it will show you how to make a plan that leads you where *you* want to go. Then it will help you follow the *action* steps necessary to achieve your goal.

As a former "I-thought-knowing-it-all-was-the-ultimate-destination-type" person, I once felt frustrated, disappointed, and unhappy with my life. And not just in one area but in many (personal, career, social). Many times I gave up and said, "It's too late. It's just too late for me. I should have, could have, would have done it, but I didn't, so that's that. And now it's too late."

I was stuck, but I didn't know why. I'd learned so much in my practice as a chiropractor working with patients. Almost daily I helped them see that knowledge alone wasn't enough, but *action* was essential for change. The irony, of course, was I could be so objective while helping my patients yet blind to my own limitations.

But it's not too late. Now is all you have. All you have is this minute, as you are reading this book. And in *this* minute you have a choice. You can throw in the towel, put down this book, and again say, "it's too late for me" or "I can't" or 'I don't know how". **OR** (this is a very big or) you can ask the questions: "What can I do to turn my life around and move in a new direction?" "How can I break free and head in a direction that will finally allow me to have more for myself and feel good at the same time?"

That's what this book can do, **IF** (this is a very big if) you take the ideas and recommendations to heart and use them in a way that's different than before. Take *action*. And don't give up. Then you'll be on the road to success, your own personal success.

Sound too easy? Well, it's not easy, but it is simple. Like anything else, it's simple when you have a plan, an outline, a recipe, or a map, and when you practice until you know not only what to do but how to do it.

So let's get started. And wait for me, I'm coming with you.

My best to you,

Jenna

Part One:
Ready?

The Man's Room

It was the beginning of a new year, some years ago, and I was feeling a little restless, feeling like I was in a rut. I needed some time off to sort out what was next for me. I decided to plan a week in March for a stay-at-home vacation. You know, do things to pamper myself– like massages and walks at the arboretum-and not schedule too much, or too heavily, so as to leave room for a movie matinee at the drop of a hat. I added one last-minute event, a visit to a life coach I knew. I was working with a self-help book about personal fulfillment. I knew the life coach used it in the classes she taught. "If I do the exercises in this book by myself I just know I'm going to go through them too fast and skip the hard parts where I should slow down and really focus. I know myself well enough to know I am going to take shortcuts, and if I do, I might miss out on the benefits." I could hear my father saying, "If you are going to do it, do it right or don't do it at all." Okay, Dad.

So I phoned Arlene "Can you help me with this? I'd like to have you lead me through the exercises in your book. I want to jumpstart my speaking career, and I need to understand how to do it."

I arrived at her office, and we got right to work. Her first question was "What do you really want in your life?" I had skimmed the questions; I knew what I was going to say—I want to have a successful speaking career. Instead what came out of my mouth was--"I want a partner." Pause. Did I say that? Where did that come from? I started to cry. You see, when I got divorced, I thought I'd meet someone in a few years. But two years became five, then ten, and then fifteen years. I had been a single mom all those years. I hadn't dated. I just did the Mom thing, and the Chiropractor thing and the Teacher thing.

I had even gone so far as to tell myself I was never going to have a partner. I had lots of beliefs, lots of negative self-talk, "Men don't like me, I'm not (fill in the blank)--Or I'm too (fill in the blank). I don't even want a partner anymore because I know I can't have one." It hadn't worked out too well in the romance department before, so I thought it never would.

When, "I want a partner," came out of my mouth, I was more than just surprised. I was confused. And I was really scared.

Arlene and I spent the next two hours exploring what had just been discovered. "You don't have any space in your life for a man. Look at your schedule. Look at your activities. Look at your thoughts. Everything you've been doing and are doing leaves no room, physically or psychologically, for anything new in your life, especially a man.

Eight months earlier my son had moved to Chicago after graduating from high school. My everyday single mom days were over. I was now living alone.

Then Arlene said, "Here's what I suggest--the room that was your son's, is it empty?"

"Yes."

"Well, take everything out of it. I mean everything. Don't leave one thing in it. Prime it, paint it white, and put a sign on the door that reads 'The Man's Room.' Can you do that?"

"I guess so."

"Can you do that this weekend?"

"Yeah, I guess."

"And what do you think you can do to prepare yourself to be a partner?" she asked.

"I don't know. It's been too many years, and I don't know how to be a partner," I answered. Then I came up with

4

all the reasons I couldn't be a partner and didn't know how to be one. "There aren't any men out there anyway." And then finally out of nowhere I said, "You know, I've always wanted to learn to dance."

"What about taking lessons?"

"But I don't know how to dance."

"That's why you take lessons-to learn. Could you learn to dance?"

"I guess so. Yeah, I saw an ad in the paper for an introduction to dance lessons."

"Alright, can you agree to sign up for eight lessons?"

"Sure, why not, I can do that."

So I left with my homework: create "The Man's Room" and sign up for dance lessons.

And that's just what I did for the next two days--the last two days of my vacation. I took everything out of Josh's old room, painted it white, and made a beautifully framed sign that said "The Man's Room." I hung it on the door, called the studio, and signed up for dance lessons.

Walking into that dance studio the first day scared me to death. It was all so unfamiliar, so outside of my comfort zone.

The teacher introduced himself, "Good morning, I'm Sarge."

"I'm Jenna. I want to learn how to dance. But I've got to tell you a few things first. I'm taking dance lessons to learn how to become a partner. I always lead in everything I do in my life--teaching, parenting, and doctoring. I don't know how to follow, and I'm afraid I won't be able to learn."

Sarge said "No problem. I've been teaching for almost thirty years. I can teach you how to dance, how to follow, and how to be a partner."

"Really? I don't know if that's possible, but I'm here, and I'm willing to do anything."

Everything was so different. Just being around a strong, good-looking man was different enough. There were no men in my life. And dancing the waltz and foxtrot, where you hold each other and move to the music, felt so strange. I was so nervous that I'm surprised I made it through the first lesson.

After it was over Sarge said, "You don't have any confidence. I can tell by your posture and the way you move. But don't worry, that will all change. The way you get confidence is through experience and practice. You'll do just fine."

So "The Man's Room" and the dance lessons were in place. Now I was thinking on my own. What else could I do to get things moving? I read a few books about how to meet men and how to act on a date, The Mars/Venus stuff, when to talk, and when to shut up!

And I signed up on Match.com. For those of you who don't know about internet dating, it's a place online where you meet people. You place a profile of yourself—name, age and physical attributes, your likes and dislikes, and what you're looking for (a friend, a date, a partner, a spouse). You pay for a membership by the month.

I put my profile and picture online and read through the profiles of men who met my preferences of age and location. I emailed the ones I thought I'd like to meet. I talked to a few on the phone. I met a few in person. And I dated for awhile. Mostly it ended in frustration.

But I was determined to learn how to be a good partner and to find a good partner. I was determined to learn how to dance a dance that I didn't know. So I talked to my coach again, and she made it clear, "You've got to be willing to do

6

whatever it takes to get where you want and to meet the man of your dreams."

And I said, "I'm willing."

I kept a notebook next to my computer to write down whom I had emailed, to keep track of those I got responses from, and notes about each person. One morning while thinking about all the meetings and all the subsequent disappointments, I wrote in my notebook in huge red letters, "I QUIT!" The message was for God. You see I had already yelled at God: "Where is he? I think there's someone out there. Hurry up already! Why is this taking so long?"

Though I had written, "I QUIT," I still had two more weeks on my membership. So I said, "Alright, it couldn't hurt to send out just one more batch of messages." Like cookies, I sent out batches. And so I did. I sent out fifteen little notes. "Hi, I saw your profile, you sound nice. Check out my profile and please write to me if you think I sound nice, too." And I got a reply from just one person, screen name Easygowin." The reason I had written to Easygowin was because of one specific line in his profile that said, "I always wanted to learn to ballroom dance, but I never had a partner." I wrote to him; he wrote back. We corresponded for a few weeks talking about our past, our children, our hopes and, of course, about dancing. After that, we talked on the phone for a few weeks and then we met at 2:06 pm on a Saturday at the Starbucks. We talked for hours. It was like at first sight.

Easygowin's real name is Ed. And we talked and saw each other a lot in the next few weeks. It turns out he was moving. He was thinking of moving to either Costa Rica or Pennsylvania.

So, I mentioned "The Man's Room."

"Would it help you to put a few things in 'The Man's Room'?" I asked casually.

"Uh, what do you mean, what's 'the man's room'?" Ed asked.

"Well, I have this room that has nothing in it that you could use if it would help."

To make this story a little shorter - three weeks later Ed moved his stuff and himself into "The Man's Room." It was just short of nine months, and I had found my partner.

Now you've heard my favorite story. It shows how I followed what is outlined in this book, and now I'm living with the results happily ever after.

That's enough about me. This book is about you. Let's look at how you can use the same methods and strategies I did to get what you've always wanted.

This is a good place to start—right here and right now.

8

I have spent my days stringing
and unstringing my instrument
while the song I came
to sing remains unsung.

Rabindranath Tagore

Chapter One
What Do YOU Want?

Now let's focus on what you want. Don't worry how you are going to get it. What's important is your intention. Here's an example: When my son was four years old, he told me the car was really dirty. I suggested we wash it. He countered with, "Why don't we throw it away and get a new one?"

"That's a great idea! We're not going to do that but that's a great idea," I replied with equal enthusiasm.

It was a great idea. Not a practical one, or a financially sound one, but a great one nonetheless from a four-year-old! The intention was to have a clean car, and if we threw the dirty one away and got a new one, then it would be clean, at least for a while.

What you have in mind may not be practical or financially sound either. You may have no idea how you would actually get there, but that's not what this first question is about. It's about *what* do you want? Like when you were a kid and someone asked you what you wanted to be when you grew up, and you answered the first thing that came into your mind that moment.

You see, we've got two separate minds that don't necessarily agree with each other. We have a subconscious mind and a conscious mind. They're both on duty all the time; however, it's the conscious mind that stands guard at the door that leads to the subconscious. The conscious mind is the one that, like the bouncer at a club, wants to see some ID before you'll be able to get in. The subconscious would let anybody in anytime, anyhow, anywhere.

What has this got to do with what you want? If you focus on *what* first, you can sneak past the conscious mind. When we look at the *how* later, we'll have to ask permission from the conscious about how to do what we want. Get it?

This is like wishful thinking, in a way. So, let me ask the question again: what do you *really* want? If you have your answer already, that's great. Write it here:

_____

No answer yet? That's okay, too. Then let's ask the question another way: what is it you really wanted at some other time but you took that desire and suppressed it, or hid it away, or rejected it because you thought it was impractical,

12

difficult, or impossible? Yes, that's the one. Write it here:

Still nothing? That's okay. You'll have another chance later. Just stay with me.

Don't censor your wishes and dreams. You see, we all have an ongoing dialogue with our thoughts all day long, from morning until the wee hours. We're always talking to ourselves. It's a running commentary on what we are doing, with whom, how, and on and on and on. A lot of this commentary is negative. What you can't do, why you can't, bringing up evidence from the past and reminding yourself of every slip-up and error you ever made. This conversation tends to get extremely loud when you start to think about beginning something new.

My self-talk made it hard for me to sit down at the keyboard this morning. It went something like this: "I guess I'll get started on my book."

"You're going to write a book?" my critical voice yelled at me from across the room. "You? Who are you kidding? You don't know how. You've never done this before. You are going to bomb sister, and you know it. Give up now and save your self a lot of time and trouble. Stick with what you already do, kiddo. Go give someone a lumbar adjustment!"

"Be quiet," I replied with all the patience I could muster. "I had the same conversation with you when I was in chiropractic school about how I wouldn't be able to do it, and again when I was looking for the man of my dreams. You've stopped me before, but you can't stop me for good. So let's just cut to the chase. I'm going to do this."

You win some, you lose some. I won that round.

The only way to overcome that kind of inner dialogue is to recognize your negative self-talk and confront it. Trying to ignore it, which might seem easier, just doesn't work.

Where to Look for What You Want

Health. Take a look at all the areas of your life. Take an overview. Is what you really want in the area of health? Maybe there are results you have wanted forever, but you have just given up on them. Like how much you weigh? How much energy you have or don't have? Doing some physical activity you've always loved but rarely participated in? Or maybe there's an illness you've been ignoring out of fear. Something that could be helped, but you don't know how or where to get that help.

Work. What about your work or career? Have you been in a dead-end job for the last ten years and can't see any way out? Are you working at a job you like, but now it's time to move on? What did you always want to be when you grew up, but for whatever reasons you didn't take that path? Hmmm. Maybe it's a job you don't get paid for, a volunteer job you've thought about for years but still haven't gotten started.

Family Life. Are you single and want to be married? Married and want to be single? Want a baby? Are you an empty-nester and like the freedom? Maybe you're an empty-nester and its too much space. Do you have all the friends you want? Or are too many friends taking up too much time right now?

Social Life. Could you find what you really want in the area of recreation or leisure? A hobby you've never pursued, and now you have the time but not the courage? Or you could explore some outlet for creativity and enjoyment?

Or maybe it's in the area of **Finances**? Or **Education**? Or **Spirituality**?

Here's a good place to make a list of three things you really want for yourself. Not like a new outfit complete with Victoria's Secret matching underwear, or a new dining room set. But things you know will make a difference in *the quality of your life now and into the distant future.*

Before you start writing, stop. Close your eyes. Take three long, deep, and relaxing breaths. Exhale each one slowly and let your mind wander. Just let it go. Use your imagination: You're tiptoeing around wanting to take a peek at your list of things you really want. Maybe it's hidden on a sheet of paper in a locked drawer in a hidden room in a deserted mansion. Or maybe it's clearly in huge red letters on a big billboard along the highway. Use your imagination. Look and see what's there for you. Now write your list down.

1. _____

2. _____

3. _____

What Do YOU Want?

One way to limit yourself is by never selecting just one thing to focus on. Say there are five or ten or twenty things you want, and you can't seem to prioritize. Then you might never have any of them. By selecting one, your odds of being successful increase tremendously. But then there are the old doubts that creep in and say, "You don't want to select just one. Look at what you'll be missing out on with all the other options. Keep your options open, baby. Yeah, that's the way; keep all your options open!" And you wind up with *bubkas*, the Yiddish word for nothing! That's what you get when you keep all your options open and never get around to closing in on one.

I read somewhere: "You can't have it all." And somewhere else I heard, "You can have it all, just not at the same time!" I don't know if we can have it all or not, but the chances of getting what we want go way up when we go for one major goal at a time!

Do you think this focus on a single item from your list might be a little limiting when it comes to what you want and need in the future? You bet it is, but as I've already said, that's a good thing!

I don't suggest using the past as an indicator of the future, because it's hazardous, except with your successes! The past does not predict the future. The logical mind says that it does. But we don't want to play with the logical mind right now, remember? The logical mind just looks for cold, hard evidence and finds it anywhere it can and says, "See, I told you so. You can't do it." Instead we want to use our imagination to look at what we really want.

And then there are all those emotions. Emotions have a way of interfering with identification of your needs. Remember the negative self-talk I mentioned? Well, if you add a soundtrack of strong emotions to that self-talk, you are almost guaranteed not to move in any new direction. Take some guilt, add some strong feelings of shame or disappointment, and sprinkle in a dash of fear, and you ain't going anyplace new!

That's where self-esteem comes in. The way you talk to yourself, plus the way you feel at the time, determines where you are on the self-esteem scale. If you don't have very high regard for yourself, then you won't believe in yourself or your talents and skills. You won't be able to make the best choices.

What Do YOU Want?

Beliefs can either limit or expand our ability to grow. What you believe colors everything. What you believe affects who you are, what you do, what you have, and how far you can go. It even affects how others see you. For example, my high school friend Susan always had a date on Friday nights. She wasn't the most popular or the prettiest girl around, but many times over the years, I heard her say "There are so many available boys. There is no shortage of nice guys to date. I never have a problem getting dates." Which came first—her *belief* in the abundance of boys and dates or the boys and dates? Make a note of this; it's invariably the belief that produces the outcome.

My conversation with myself regarding guys was just the opposite. In my belief system there weren't any good ones, and they weren't going to like me anyway. You guessed it; I didn't have many dates in high school. This belief stuff is not rocket science, but it is subtle. Until we clearly recognize what we believe about ourselves and the world around us, we are at the mercy of those beliefs.

Change your mind, and you change your reality! It's simple. But it's not easy. Oh, no, it's not easy. It takes awareness first and then action. Being open, receptive, and

19

flexible will help you turn around. How do you do that you may ask? Good question. But for now, just put it in your pocket. We'll answer this question in Chapters 5 and 6.

Pick just one item from your "Most Wanted" list on page 16. Just one. It doesn't matter which one you choose: You can choose the one with the health goal in it, or the man of your dreams, or financial freedom, or inner peace. What *is* important is making a choice. Pick the one that really matters to you, the one that would give you the most satisfaction upon completion. Yes, that one. Pick that one, and write it here:

Don't throw the others away, just put them aside for now. Once you get the hang of this you will start accomplishing goals on the list faster and faster because now you've acquired a critical mass of evidence that you can succeed. You will become someone who gets where you want to go. As your beliefs about yourself start to change, the process speeds up because there is less guilt and fear and doubt. Instead of coming up with *bubkas*, you'll find you have *mazel,* the Yiddish word for luck.

20

What Do YOU Want?

When a new patient comes to my office, the first question I ask is, "What is your main complaint? What do you want to change?" My patients usually want relief from headaches, backaches, or stiff necks.

In this chapter we've made a list of your life-changing goals (what you want) and narrowed it to a single one to provide a starting point. You're now on your way.

The questions in Chapter 2 relate to your history. What has happened in your past that contributes to your complaint? We'll think about how you got where you are now and how that relates to what you want but don't yet have.

If you haven't picked your one focus and written it in the space on the previous page, then do that before moving to the next chapter. You want it to work this time, remember?

Even monkeys fall out of trees.

Japanese Proverb

Chapter 2
Your History

You know the illustration about a glass of water described by some as half full and others as half empty? The one used to demonstrate whether a person has a positive or negative point of view? "Yes," you say with a sigh, "it's so overused, please, don't use that one again!"

We're not looking at either/or this time. Let's look at both: the glass is half full *and* the glass is half empty. We want to explore both points of view. In this chapter we'll look at the fullness of the glass. What do you have already? (In Chapter 3 we'll consider the half-empty glass, and explore what's missing). For now, we want to examine your objective history, and as Sgt. Joe Friday used to say on *Dragnet,* "The facts ma'am, just the facts."

Until we acknowledge our personal history we will probably repeat it. From the moment that we're born, everything that happens to us, everything we hear or say, and maybe every thought we have is recorded in our own personal "hard drive." And when we look back and take inventory of our past, our memory provides us with evidence of whom and how we've been. Unfortunately, memories are not entirely accurate.

Our perspective changes from the time something happens until the present, and the emotions involved with the experience are not usually remembered accurately either. There's a tendency for us to see our lives as a continuum, an evolution of what was, flowing forward into what is, and moving right along into what will be. Here's the rub. There is only NOW. Right NOW. This instant. The past doesn't exist any longer. Not really. The future doesn't either, even if your date book says it does. So right now is the only place where you have the power to choose. Right now is where you can decide if what you've done is valuable. I'm asking you to look back from where you are now. Look back to assess your history and identify things you've done in the past that can be of benefit to you in the future. I want you to pack your bag for your next trip with all the things that will help you in getting what you want.

Modus operandi means "a way of doing or accomplishing something." One person does everything in a neat, orderly fashion, another works quickly, another meticulously, and yet another flies by the seat of her pants! There is no right or

24

wrong *modus operandi;* it's a matter of whether it gets you where you want to go and with the outfits you want to wear!

Who you are speaks volumes: what you've done, and haven't done; where you've been and haven't been; what you've asked for, what you've been afraid of, what you risked, and where you backed off--all say important things about you. However, what actually happens when we take this kind of inventory for ourselves is that we seem to throw in a lot of judgment. "I didn't finish college. And because of that I'm lazy or fickle or a dozen other judgmental conclusions." If you are objective, you just state the fact: "I didn't finish college." Period. End of conversation. See what I mean? Let's just gather evidence and not say whether the facts are good or bad, OK? We get stuck in all our negative judgments about what happened, and this keeps us from moving forward.

What are you good at? What are your strongest skills: education, family, social, financial, personal? It's the kind of things you share early in a conversation when you meet a new person. You say something like, I have a master's degree...I never got my high school diploma...I'm a great dancer...I'm always tripping over my own feet...I never seem to have enough money to do what I want…I'm great at making a budget and following through.

What's important about how we see ourselves is we get stronger and stronger in the areas where we have confidence and tend to neglect the qualities that are more difficult for us. The things we want but don't have usually lie in areas where we have less confidence and less experience. The only way to gain confidence is through experience. The only way to get experience is by taking action. One way to take successful action is to know what you want, what you already have, and what areas need improvement.

Where are your talents and skills? Is it academics, business, or athletics? And don't forget to look at parenting, household management, hobbies, and communications as well. Everyone has special talents. Yes, everyone. A talent can be a knack or a skill that seems to come easily. And because it seems easy, you may discount it. A friend of mine is a great cook. For twenty years she has created wonderful menus and produced delicious meals every night, but because she doesn't work outside the home and collect a paycheck for these meals, she does not necessarily consider what she does a talent or

26

creative skill. Because it's easy for her, she does not see it as valuable. Isn't it wonderful that some things come easily?

What fascinates you? An area of fascination can lead to a talent waiting to blossom. (A good example is Anne Clark's story, in the introduction to Part Two.) Look at things you collect or hobbies you enjoy. What are books and movie themes that attract you?

Where have you already been successful? What are you good at? Stop and think about it for a minute before you read on. Write down several areas:

1. _____

2. _____

3. _____

4. _____

5. _____

Don't overlook areas that are so easy or so routine that they might seem insignificant. Are you successful at getting up and dressed and going to work on time every morning? Are you successful at maintaining friendships over years through thick and thin? Are you successful at earning money? Are you successful at driving a car as shown by your accident-free record? Are you a successful parent? Did you include anything mentioned in this paragraph in your list above? Did you dismiss any of these areas because you thought, "it's just the way it is"? How come what you want now in your life but don't have isn't "just the way it is"? (Aha, I thought you'd like that question!)

Let's look at where habits fit in. The only time I hear the word habit is in a sentence talking about breaking a bad one. But it's good habits that make it easier for us to get things done. They are time-saving, beneficial and automatic actions that make our daily routine more efficient. A habit is something we do without thinking about it anymore because we've done it so many times.

My dance lessons are about turning the steps into good habits where I do them in the proper order with correct technique. My dance teacher says it takes 1100 repetitions for the steps to become a habit! When the steps are automatic, I can fully enjoy the music and my partner.

Bad habits are also automatic. That's what they have in common with the good ones. The difference is these so called "bad habits" allow us to deny, avoid, waste or divert our energy. We are given so much time in a day. If we invest our

28

time in those activities and people we enjoy- ahhhh. If we waste our time by automatically doing things that have no benefit or purpose in our life--uh oh!

What are *your* habits? What do you do that may have been enjoyable once, but isn't anymore? Eating? Shopping? Smoking? Drinking? Gambling? Sudoku? We'll look closely at these areas in Chapter 4.

Now here's a really good question: What have you left incomplete from your past? Incompletes are possible successes that didn't get finished. Oh, you thought those were failures. Well, they're not. They are just incompletes. You don't know whether the undertaking succeeded or failed, but because it is unfinished, you say it failed! Something got in the way of achieving your goal or hitting the target. Perhaps some unexpected circumstance interrupted your plan; then fear crept in and stopped you for good. Maybe fear of failure *or* fear of success. Not completing a goal keeps it vague, uncertain, and unsettling. That's the exact opposite of what you'll do when you make your plan. You see, being vague and uncertain, even in a few areas, creates vague and uncertain anxiety about nothing in particular and everything in general. Vagueness keeps you in a state of stressful anticipation, only you don't

29

know exactly what the feeling is about. Anxiety and stress will rob you of the energy you need to complete the thing you want to do.

Granted, sometimes there are extraordinary challenges. People are born with health problems or born into poverty or born into an abusive family. From all I've read and heard, those challenges can be perfect springboards to go way beyond what a person might normally accomplish. In any extraordinary challenge the situation can be a stop or a detour or a taking-off point. The outcome results from your point of view, from how you handle what comes your way; how you play the hand you're dealt. Some people have more challenges than others in a lifetime. Some people only seem to have more challenges because theirs are visible to others.

Gwen was a person who had challenges from the moment she was born. Her mother died during her birth, and she almost didn't survive. As a result of birth trauma Gwen had cerebral palsy which created physical challenges, including the need for a wheelchair and difficulty with speech. Gwen was also an African-American woman with limited income. Sound like three strikes? Read on.

When I met Gwen she was in her early twenties, living with her strong, loving grandmother who had raised her. She had a college degree, and she was preparing to attend a six-day "ropes" course. The ropes course included three events: the zip-line, the rappel, and the Tyrolean traverse. Each event involved being rigged up by ropes to equipment that allows a person to either go from the top of a mountain to the bottom on an incline or straight down the side of a mountain, or from one mountain top to another pulling hand over hand. Phew!

Gwen couldn't do these events on her own, but she could with the help of a trainer accompanying her. Gwen had courage and courage is the ability to use your heart and your spirit to overcome fear: False Evidence Appearing Real. She had been climbing internal mountains all her life and she had a grandmother who taught her she could do anything she set her mind to.

Whether you consider something a challenge or a problem or a possibility depends on your perception. We learn our perceptions at an early age from those around us. It's our way of seeing the world, our vantage point, our position in life. Consider the child who falls down but isn't hurt. He immediately looks at his parent's face and seeing fear and

YES, IT *IS* ALL ABOUT YOU

anxiety, starts to cry. The experience changed from a neutral event to the perception that it *should* be painful or fearful.

Gwen's grandmother told her she could do lots of things other people in similar situations thought were impossible. They couldn't go to college, climb mountains or win the Special Olympics in wheelchair racing at the state level! Gwen perceived herself as someone who was capable of meeting challenges and being successful. Her self-esteem was healthy.

People will help you or hinder you on your journey. Maybe you've heard reference to "toxic people"--those people who aren't good for you. They might be called friends, but they don't support you, love you, listen to you, or act like a friend. In other words they are in your life because you allow them to be. Okay, okay, it may happen to be your mother who's the toxic person! Well, you are still in charge of your boundaries. Boundaries are the perimeters *you* set in terms of how people treat you. If you stay on the phone for an hour when the person on the other end is "yelling and dumping," then your boundaries are misplaced.

Let's look at people who have helped you. Recognize who specifically and what kind of person generally has been helpful to you. Some of us like having our hand held every step of the way. Others just want someone to lean on from time to time. Which kind of help works best for you? There is no *right* way, only what works for you. Make a list of people from the past and present who you can count on to support you in your new venture:

_____   _____

_____   _____

_____   _____

_____   _____

There are always people available to help and guide and mentor us. What? Some of you doubt this? Those of you who are saying, "No, there aren't," may have issues allowing people to love and support you. Many of us were taught that we have to do everything for ourselves. Some of us believe (there are those beliefs again) that it's a sign of weakness and failure if we ask for or receive help from others. For now, if you know how to give support— and I bet you do— then all you have to do is learn how to receive. See, you're already halfway there!

What you have identified in this chapter are your successes, your talents, your incompletes, your helpers, and your obstacles (those who make your life difficult). And you now have an awareness of what you want.

In the next chapter we'll look at what you still need. What do you need to get around detours? What beliefs (your way of thinking) have brought you to where you are today? What are your challenges and obstacles? What keeps you stuck? What will get you to move?

If you wait for tomorrow,
tomorrow comes.
If you don't wait for tomorrow,
tomorrow comes.

Senegalese Proverb

Chapter 3
What Do YOU Need?

All you have to do is observe children in the act of being themselves. This is how they are, especially at a younger age: uninhibited, flexible and there always seems to be an abundance of movement. Children don't like restrictions. They like to run, play, make noise, and move freely from one place to another, from one physical posture to another. They might watch television upside down with their head hanging over the arm of the chair. It doesn't look very comfortable to most of us, but if you ask, you'll hear, "Oh, yeah, this is great. I like it." And their emotions move just as quickly. When they don't like something or can't have their way, they might yell, "I hate you," which can be interpreted by a smart parent as, "I'm angry" and ten minutes later their response is, "I love you," which can be interpreted by a wise parent as, "Thank you."

As we get older and more socialized, we're asked to change less and move less. But movement is necessary for change. We have to learn how to move better or differently to move around challenges, through situations, or away from or towards other situations. In order to change outcomes, we have to move away from the outcomes we don't want and towards a solution. That's easier said than done, and it doesn't take an Einstein to realize this. What Albert Einstein did say was, "Nothing happens until something moves." Was he talking about molecules and atoms, or was he talking about you getting on the exercise bike for thirty minutes on Tuesday mornings?

So the first step in overcoming a challenge is to know movement is necessary and change is essential. At the very least you must be willing to entertain the possible need for movement. That movement could be a physical one, a change in your emotional state or a shift in your beliefs. Somewhere in yourself and in your life, you will need to move. That's how you get from where you are now to where you want to be--you move.

Movement starts in your imagination and in your thoughts. Before you get up to get a drink of water, you first have a thought about being thirsty. Or maybe you have a fleeting image of getting a glass, filling it, and drinking it. It's all so fast that we don't realize the action did not come first. We have an idea first, and then we act if we are going to change anything. We first need change in our minds. Women are

38

always being told they change their minds. However, I'm talking about change at a deeper level: changing our minds at the level of beliefs and perceptions about who we are, what we can achieve, and what we can have in our lives.

Change means you cause or allow something to be different. Here's the catch: we say, "I wish things were different" and in the same breath we say, "Oh, but I don't like change!" Which is it? BOTH. And guess what? Everything changes anyway. It's a reality of life.

So what we're really saying is "I want to be in control of the way things change. I want to have a say in it. I don't want to be the victim of changes that just happen." Well here's the good news: you *can* be in control. You just have to show up with all of your energy and intentions and plans in hand. You have to say what you want to change and then allow it to happen, at the same time being open and flexible to whatever unplanned changes may come along as well.

Everyone takes the limits of his
own vision for the limit of the world.
Arthur Schopenhauer

YES, IT *IS* ALL ABOUT YOU

Imagine everyone is wearing a different pair of sunglasses. Each pair has different colored lenses. The pair you have on allows you to see through a beautiful shade of sea-foam green. Sea-foam green is your perception, your point of view. But you think everyone else is also seeing through the same green tint. You can't tell with your own glasses on, can you? And everyone else thinks the same about the colored glasses they're wearing, too.

We each have our own perceptions and don't even realize it. For example, if you perceive the world to be a friendly place, the world will give you evidence that supports your belief. Oh sure, there will be times when unfriendly things happen, but they don't make the same impression on you because it is now the exception rather than the rule.

We have to be able to imagine what we want. Let's look at children again. They have wonderful imaginations. We were once children. *Ergo* we have wonderful imaginations. They are rusty imaginations perhaps. They are probably hidden and most likely dreadfully out of shape but nonetheless existent. See what I mean? Come on, use your imagination!

Do I hear any of you saying, "But I don't have a good imagination"? Maybe what you mean is, "I don't have a good *positive* imagination." Here's the difference: every time you focus on the obstacles, problems, or excuses you are using your imagination to produce more of the same. And you are using your energy and efforts to imagine the outcome that you don't want, rather than the one you do want.

Obstacles are part of every journey, allowing you to use your creativity and find solutions you wouldn't have found otherwise. Taking paths you wouldn't otherwise have thought to take may ultimately make the outcome better.

Talk about an obstacle! Over thirty years ago I was robbed in someone's home while babysitting. At the time I had a degree in psychology, was recently married, and didn't have a clue about what to do with the rest of my life. After that terrifying event, I felt compelled to spend months soul-searching, looking for the purpose of my life. Within the year I knew I wanted to become a chiropractic physician. This was not a path I would have ever imagined myself taking previously.

There are also special circumstances that don't come from your imagination. A physical disability or health challenge could be one of them. You might have been born into a family where race, class, financial status, or educational opportunities did not provide the same opportunities as someone else. Alcoholism or an abusive living environment may be part of your picture. These are all places where some people have made their start, but it is not the place where anyone has to stay. There are many reasons and many excuses why someone might remain in a bad situation; however, there are many more stories of people who have come from challenges like these and not only survived but thrived. Not only thrived but inspired others with their life stories. Remember Gwen and the ropes course? I am inspired every time I think of her.

When I was twelve years old I finished second in the eighth grade spelling bee. Minda came in first. I misspelled the word facetious. I spelled it V-I-C-I-O-U-S. I'd never heard the word facetious before. That's what happened. End of story.

Somehow I changed the story in my mind, and I no longer just remembered what happened. When I retold it to myself it was about how I never came in first in anything, always second. It was about how I wasn't good enough almost anywhere in life. Come on! I didn't know how to spell facetious. Period. All the rest of the story was my memory being creative in a very negative way!

What Do YOU Need?

So what you believe about who you are and what you're able to do is the best and only place to start. Remember, "Just the facts, ma'am." Sometimes you aren't aware of your negative thoughts. So if you feel there's an area of your life, or several areas, where you never win, work backwards until you identify the source or sources of your negative thinking and expectations.

For example, let's say for the last ten years you've said you want a new, different, and better job. It hasn't happened. Perhaps you believe:

A. I don't deserve a new job

B. I couldn't have a better job

C. There are no better jobs

D. It is too hard to find a better job

E. It wouldn't have worked anyway

F. all of the above and maybe more

First, discover what you actually believe, positive or negative. Then identify a more positive outcome and change your mind to support your new belief. A belief is an idea we think is true, but we don't have any proof. What do you believe about yourself? What do you know about yourself?

Is there a difference between what you believe and what you know?

There are tons of books written on this subject. I just wanted to make the point that you live from your beliefs. You follow your beliefs like you would a map, and then you're surprised at where you wind up. What? Surprised? It's the nature of the mind to embellish and fill in the blanks and connect the dots. The mind doesn't necessarily care if the picture is correct or incorrect.

Let's get back to you. What are your obstacles? Do you think it's too late for you? Or are your obstacles grounded in negative belief systems about yourself? Do you entertain judgments and criticisms that damage your self-esteem? Have you adopted a negative self-image from what others think and forfeited what you know to be true about yourself? Or maybe you hold yourself back by something circumstantial, like not enough money, too much weight, or a lack of education.

Although this chapter is entitled "What Do You Need?" it discusses what gets in your way, where you might get stuck, and what stops you from going after the things you want. In case it still isn't clear, this chapter asks you to identify where *you* are stopped and to begin looking for solutions.

44

What Do YOU Need?

Before you go on, list the beliefs, perceptions, and circumstances you use *most* to limit yourself:

1. _____
2. _____
3. _____
4. _____
5. _____

Maybe you're like my Dad. He said that what limited him was not having "oomph." Near the end of his life, he confessed that he always wanted to be a doctor but hadn't tried. The reasons he gave were that his mother died when he was young and he had to quit school to help support the family and his family was poor. When he looked back on his life at age seventy-five, however, he said the *real* reason he never became a doctor was that he just didn't have oomph.

Oomph equals motivation. What keeps you from staying motivated? We're going to look at that in Chapter 8.

www.Jenna.Eisenberg.com

Part Two:
Get Set!

The Anne Clark Story and More

Let me tell you about Anne Clark. She used to teach fitness classes at the YMCA and run five miles everyday. Some of you may be thinking, "So what? I do that, or I know someone who does that, too. What's the big deal?" Well the big deal is Anne Clark was eighty-seven years old at the time.

At age sixty-two she retired as a schoolteacher. She had bursitis and, arthritis, and she was depressed. She said, "I don't know how much longer I have to live, but I know I don't want to live it feeling like this." She said the most exercise she had ever done was vacuuming her living room. Deciding she needed to do something; she joined the "Y" and signed up for a walking class. She walked regularly for over a year. Then she started to jog. She jogged short races, then longer ones. When she started running it was short races working up to marathons. Anne held marathon records in her age group and her picture has been on the cover of Runner's World *magazine. Anne's husband used to sew and made outfits for her to run in. She was the best dressed runner around, too.*

She wasn't willing to listen to the voice in her mind that said she was too old or too sick. Was she exceptional? You bet. She was exceptional in her commitment to herself and to life and to not letting herself stay stopped. Along with physical exercise, she exercised her ability to overcome the attitudes that limited her.

She listened to her positive self and took steps, one at a time. She started exercising but she also changed her diet taking out what she called the three W's--white sugar, white flour, and white salt. Most importantly, she changed her mind by listening to her positive self and not believing she was too old, too sick, or too tired to make changes.

YES, IT *IS* ALL ABOUT YOU

A few years ago Anne died. She was ninety-six years of age. Her memorial service was overflowing with hundreds of people who she had inspired, in her words, "Keep the bod moving." Her son shared her life story with everyone at the service. When he finished, he told us there would be refreshments in the church basement. He also told us we would find a long table holding all the medals and trophies and ribbons his mother had won over the years. He invited each of us to take one home in memory of Anne. There was a collective gasp when he made this offer. And then he laughed saying "What am I going to do with a whole roomful of her awards?" So we all went "shopping" for our memento, our award.

I share my story about Anne Clark because I have been inspired by Anne for over twenty-five years, and I love to tell her story. The gold medallion I took as my memento reminds me to "keep on keepin' on" in each new endeavor. Now that you know her story, you can have her in your corner, too.

Abraham Maslow originated a theory in psychology about the hierarchy of humans needs. Stated in simple words it says we must fill our basic needs (like food, shelter and safety) before we can even begin to think about taking care of our higher needs (like fulfilling hopes and dreams). Survival is necessary before self-actualization can occur! Beyond survival other supporting needs must also be met before we can continue our growth.

50

Let me introduce a concept called the Health Triangle. This idea is a basic tenet of chiropractic philosophy formulated by D.D. Palmer in the late 1800's. Over the years, I have modified it for my own use.

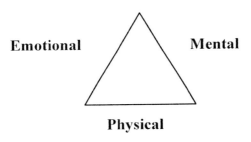

Emotional   **Mental**

Physical

Figure 1. The Health Triangle

In the diagram each of the sides is labeled: the physical (includes the muscles, bones and body chemistry); the emotional (having to do with feelings); and the mental (pertaining to thoughts, beliefs and the intellect). This is the model I use to identify and determine the needs of each person who comes into my office. I look at what they already have and what they still need.

In the next three chapters we'll look at the sides of the health triangle, one at a time. We'll be working to determine what side is your strongest, where you need the most development, and how your history affects each side. We'll see if there is interference in any of these areas and figure out what to do about it. Overall, it's the balance of the emotional, mental, and physical factors that create the foundation needed for good health and personal growth.

Interference

Interference can occur in any one or all three sides of the health triangle. Interference causes detours, but detours are not dead-ends unless you stop. They are just interference. Like static on a radio. Like a thunderstorm at a picnic. Interference is a stop only if you allow it to be one. Interference is what gets in the way of the natural order of things.

What can you do about interference? You can try to avoid it, go around it, ignore it, resist it, or analyze it. But those tactics don't work. The only thing to do is to remove the interference. You have to remove it, like fidgeting with the radio until the static is gone, or taking a pebble out of your shoe so your foot doesn't hurt. And then you must substitute something beneficial, removing what's harmful and adding what's beneficial. Sounds good, huh? It is good.

Good health is the foundation for pursuing your dreams and goals. Pursuing dreams and achieving goals is the hallmark of a life well-lived. The starting point for reaching your dreams is putting your whole system in balance.

This is the "behind the scenes" that supports the action of the play, your life. Before the curtain rises there are years of work that must be completed first. The play has to be written and published. A producer must provide the money and other resources needed. The director and then the crew and cast must be hired, trained, and rehearsed. Each has to do his or her specific job alone and as a group before opening night becomes a reality.

All the behind the scenes preparation has to be complete before you can achieve a life-long dream or reach the goal that is waiting for you in the wings. By strengthening the physical, emotional and mental aspects of yourself you will have the strength and energy needed to take action. If one or more areas are not addressed you might overextend, even exhaust, yourself as you pursue your goals. If you burn out before you get there, what have you gained?

This section of the book is about strengthening all three sides of the triangle before you begin your journey *and* maintaining that vitality as you go along. You need a strong foundation to provide the energy to progress. Maybe you have three sides that need work. Maybe only two need improvement. Chances are you've got a stronger side, a weaker side, and a so-so side. We tend to keep making our strong side stronger because that's where we have the most experience and confidence, and we avoid working on our weaker side because we *lack* experience and confidence there! Let's see what's behind your scenes as we make preparations to stage *your* play!

Eighty percent of life is just showing up.

Woody Allen

Chapter 4
The Physical Side
Strength and Vitality

The first place we will look is easiest to see--the physical body. That's where we have the clearest evidence of what's working and what's not. Imagine that we are going to take a three-week summer road trip to Yosemite Park in an RV and we need to prepare before we set out. We need the RV, we need gas and other fluids for it, and we need some maps to show us where we are going and how to get there.

The RV represents our physical body.

The physical body is our vehicle and our home. It carries us through life. Without a body we have no place to live and no way to get anywhere!

Interference to the body of the RV might look like this:

A dent in the fender.

Rust around the edges.

A tail light that doesn't work.

Poor acceleration.

A flat tire.

Your body has certain requirements before it can work properly. The following is a list of positive activities some people tend to ignore or rebel against:

1. Eating nutritious foods.
2. Getting adequate rest.
3. Doing enough exercise.
4. Drinking plenty of water.

This is a list of activities some people tend to overdo:

1. Drinking too much alcohol.
2. Smoking cigarettes.
3. Eating too much sugar.
4. Overuse/over activity.
5. Overeating.

The Past

Interference to your physical body may come from your history of experiences and may include the following things:

- A car accident
- A difficult labor and delivery (mother)
- A sports injury
- An illness or operation
- An excess of medications
- An excess of drinking/smoking/eating

The Physical Side

What interference has there been to your physical body? List instances here:

1._____

2._____

3._____

The Present

There are also everyday situations that can cause interference to a strong, balanced physical body.

- Physical exercise: overexertion or not enough activity.

- Repetitive movements in sports or work situations.

- Poor nutrition: too much alcohol, sugar; too little fresh vegetables and fruits.

- Medications.

- Inadequate rest, sleep, or relaxation.

Where is there currently interference to your physical body? List here:

1._____

2._____

3._____

Let me share a few examples of how interference to the physical and nutritional aspects of the "triangle" affects everything else.

Example 1

For many years I treated Sandy for minor neck discomfort, sometimes for headaches and every now and then for backaches. I worked with her through all the changes in balance that occur during pregnancy. Her baby was born about a month early and had some difficulty nursing. All the reflexes were not as mature as they would have been at term. However, the baby made progress, and the nursing was going well until at ten weeks old he no longer wanted to nurse from the right breast. He'd nurse like a hungry little guy from the left one but just moved his head around and wouldn't "latch" onto the right side. This caused Sandy physical discomfort along with the emotional distress of wondering what was wrong.

Remembering a similar case, I checked the baby for muscle tension in the neck and misalignment of the spine. As you know, newborns can't talk. How could I know what was wrong? I found out as soon as I touched the problem area—the baby cried. So I tapped the area gently to loosen the muscles and allow the vertebrae to move back into alignment. A restriction had made it uncomfortable for the baby to turn his head to the left, the exact movement necessary to nurse from mom's right breast. The treatment took just a few minutes from start to finish. The next feeding was better, and by the end of the day, everything was back to normal, for baby *and* mom.

Example 2

A woman in her mid-thirties complained of severe low back pain the first time she visited my office. She wanted to be well to resume her passion: playing tennis. I took a complete history of her problem referencing the health triangle. The physical pain did not come from over-use or from an accident. There didn't seem to be any structural interference. However, when I questioned her about her diet and nutrition, I discovered she drank twelve cans of soda daily. Yes, twelve cans every day! I explained to her soda was not causing the back pain directly, but each can contains seven teaspoons of sugar, and sugar has a weakening effect on all of the muscles.

I recommended she restrict her intake of soda, not cut it out entirely, because her body was used to this amount and

61

withdrawal might be uncomfortable. I suggested she cut her consumption in half.

She protested, "I can't stop drinking soda. But I can take up yoga." Was I missing something? I didn't equate doing yoga to not drinking soda. I was trying to tell her, "You are interfering with your whole system by adding this much sugar everyday. If you remove the interference it will help your back." Her response suggested she wanted to add something else that seemed easy for her, the yoga, and expected that yoga would help her system. She completely missed the point: unless the interference (sugar) was removed, there would be no improvement.

Let's get back to you. It's your turn to write down the one area from the list you made on page 59 where you could use the most improvement.

What is the most important action you can take to make this better? Write it inside the box!

We are going to include these answers in the plan you write in Chapter 7. If you have read this chapter without filling in the blanks, take another few minutes to do so now. Go on, you can do it. The next two chapters will follow the same format, but they deal with the emotional and mental sides of the triangle. Those chapters can wait patiently, if necessary, while you finish your assignment here, okay?

We don't stop laughing
because we grow old:
we grow old because we stop laughing

Author Unknown

Chapter 5
The Emotional Side
Feelings and Moods

The emotional body is the fuel. (You thought the food was the fuel, didn't you?) Food keeps the body in good working order, but what *runs* the body is our emotions. Emotions can be written as E-motions. The "E" stands for energy. Energy in motion.

Interference to your RV looks like this:

You are out of gas.

The transmission fluid is empty.

There is no windshield washer fluid.

It's not just hard to run your RV without fuel; it's impossible!

What fills us is:

1. Faith.
2. Joy.
3. Love
4. Hope.
5. Inspiration.

What depletes us is:

1. Pessimism, anxiety, or fear
2. Chronic anger or rage
3. Prolonged sadness and grief
4. Depression

Although the world is very full of suffering,
it is also full of the overcoming of it.
Helen Keller

The Past

Interference to your emotional well-being can come from a history of

- Unresolved grief from a death, divorce, another major loss
- A traumatic incident (for example a near-death experience, major illness, or post-traumatic stress from war or any catastrophic event)
- Physical/emotional/sexual/mental abuse
- Stress from past work situations

66

What is the emotional interference in your history? List it here:

1._____

2._____

3._____

The Present

Interference to your emotional well-being on a regular, on-going basis may look like these symptoms:

- Rage/anger
- Depression
- Frequent crying
- Anxiety attacks/panic attacks
- Apathy

Do you currently have emotional interference going on? If yes, list the areas:

1._____

2._____

3._____

Let's look at a couple examples where the interference may look like it's coming from the physical side, but it's really the emotions that are causing the lack of balance.

Example 1

Samuel has been coming in for "tune-ups" for years. A little adjustment to his low back, and he is usually good as new. One day he mentioned he had been diagnosed with pancreatitis, inflammation of the pancreas. He described how extremely painful it was and told me he'd experienced this pain many times, especially while traveling. He traveled to Europe frequently for business and family reasons. The problem persisted after many months of medical tests and drugs, and he had reached the point where his doctors told him there was nothing left to do.

I asked if he was willing to try hypnosis, explaining hypnosis as an easy, relaxing method to let go of emotional stress. He said he was willing, and, by the way, twenty years ago he had stopped smoking after only one treatment with the use of hypnosis. Was he going to be a good subject!

I asked him questions about the nature of his pain and when it occurred. Each answer led me to another question. We finally arrived at a point where Samuel told me he found and married the love of his life at the age of sixty-seven. But he continued to brood about the thirty-two years he spent with his first wife, how painful those years were, and how angry he was about having 'wasted' the past. Essentially, he was still spending time stuck in the old relationship. He had another issue. His father was old and ill. On two occasions Samuel had terrible bouts of pain while on the way to visit him. Samuel's underlying issues turned out to be anger with his father and his ex-wife.

With Samuel, I saw a strong connection between the physical symptoms of inflammation and pain in the pancreas and his history of anger with family members. We did a therapeutic hypnosis session where I guided him through a body relaxation and then gave him permission to let go of the pain and grievances from his past.

The pancreas is the organ that controls the level of blood sugar. On a purely symbolic level it has to do with how much sweetness there is in one's life and if that sweetness is appreciated. I suggested he fully enjoy the "sweetness" of his present and future life.

We did two hypnosis sessions; Samuel had no more episodes of pancreatitis. When I asked about his anger, he responded, "Oh, that. It's gone." He said it as if it had been nothing! It *was* nothing now, but it sure hadn't been before.

Example 2

Larry is one of my many favorite patients. It's been almost twenty years since our first meeting. He's had some physical problems with his back and knees, and an adjustment every two to three months always helps. He's also gotten relief from dietary changes made throughout the years.

His wife of thirty-five years died recently and he called for an appointment saying he couldn't stop crying. When he came in he wanted to know if I thought his feelings and emotions were normal. I told him, "There is no normal with grief. It shows up in many different ways." We talked, and I reassured him that his responses, although painful, were not unusual under the circumstances. I referred him to a counselor for help with the inevitable readjustment he was enduring.

One year passed. His first year alone was filled with significant dates: birthdays, holidays, and anniversaries. The first anniversary of his wife's death was coming up. Larry came in with minor aches and pains in three or four places. I told him he wasn't experiencing three or four different things but only one: he was still grieving, and the loss of his beloved wife was still hurting him.

He started to cry, informing me he had not come in expecting to cry or talk about grief. My response was, "Crying is a release of pain. It helps at times when nothing else will." He didn't like what I said, but he finally agreed. Then just before he left the room, he mentioned he had a cough he couldn't shake. I asked if there was anything he needed to get off his chest maybe something he hadn't said to anyone, but needed to get off his chest. He said, "I'm very lonely. I'm so lonely, and I can't talk to anyone." And again he cried. I told him he was still grieving, and as bad as it felt, he would probably not feel this way forever.

I reassured Larry that although he wasn't there yet, he would be ready to move to a more comfortable place in the future. A place where he would be ready to move on and interested in meeting someone else. I told him about how my parents had been happily married for fifty-three years and how, after my mom died, my father grieved the loss of his wonderful wife. Although he was seventy-three years old and not

71

"looking" for anyone, he found a new and different and equally wonderful woman with whom he enjoyed the last two years of his life. Larry left with a glimmer of hope, the antidote for almost any problem.

So now it's time to choose the one area you think you need the most change emotionally. Check the list on page 67 to find your answer. Please write it here:

_____

What is the one most important thing you can do in this area to improve your situation? Write it inside the box.

I know you can't wait to go on but please complete this chapter first as we will include it with our plan in Chapter 7. OK? Thanks.

Good judgment comes from experience.
Experience comes from bad judgment.

Source Unknown

Chapter 6
The Mental Side
Thoughts, Attitudes and Beliefs

Your thinking guides you on your trip. You've got the RV, and it's all fueled up and properly serviced. Now where are you going, and how do you get there? Ah, that's the real purpose of this book. We want to make sure you have the RV, the fuel, and a solid plan so you can complete your trip successfully.

Interference with navigation looks like this:

> You've lost the compass.
>
> Your cell phone dies.
>
> Your computer locks up.
>
> Or you haven't even got a map!

As a result you won't be able to navigate.

The following is a list of activities that support good mental balance:

1. Eating nutritious foods.
2. Getting adequate rest.
3. Regular exercise.
4. Drinking plenty of water.
5. Meditation and prayer.

Here's a list of behaviors that might cause mental interference:

1. Too much television.
2. Addictive behaviors.
3. Insomnia.
4. Long-term physical illness.
5. Negative or self-limiting beliefs.

The Past

Mental interference might be:

- A history of abuse.

- Any traumatic or life-threatening event.

- Ongoing situations that are mentally debilitating or very stressful.

- Negative or self-limiting beliefs as discussed in Chapter 3.

Are there patterns of interference to your thinking in your history? If, yes, list instances here:

1._____

2._____

3._____

The Present

Interference to your mind on an everyday basis might look like this:

- Confusion
- Spaciness
- Chronic procrastination
- Mental exhaustion
- Indecisiveness

Do you have everyday situations that keep you from thinking clearly? If yes, list them here:

1._____

2._____

3._____

Example

Many years ago a two-year-old named John was brought to my office for chiropractic care. He had a stiff neck, and he said, "It hurts." As he sat on the table, I did the examination easily, and it appeared he had a simple strained muscle. I asked John, "Would it be alright with you if I do a treatment so you will feel better when you wake up tomorrow morning"? He immediately replied, "Otay."

I did the adjustment. As he got off the table he said he was fine and the next day his mother reported that the neck pain was gone.

My point is John did not have the mental interference that many adults have. He wasn't asking himself a multitude of questions: How long will this take to get better? How much will it cost? Will there be traffic on the way to the office? Should I be doing this anyway? What was I supposed to buy at the store on the way home? He just said "Otay," relaxed and went with the flow. Ahhhh.

So what are the thoughts and concerns that interfere with your ability to think clearly? Do you worry? Do you overanalyze? Do you get confused? Write the number one mental interference from the items you listed on the previous page:

_____

78

What is the one most important thing you can do to remove this interference and strengthen the mental side? Write it here.

We are going to include this in the plan we will make in Chapter 7. Let me remind you one more time, just for fun— please finish filling in Chapters 4, 5, and 6 before you move on to Part Three. This will allow you to be *ready* and *prepared* when you start making your plan. These qualities are good to have when you start something new. You already knew that, didn't you?

79

Part Three:
Go, GO, GO!

My Best Friend

Barbara and I were best friends in high school. We were the kind of best friends who talked on the phone every night for three hours. Today I couldn't tell you a word we said. Not a word. We met during our freshman year, and we were best friends all through high school. Barbara was about my height, and she had naturally straight, long blonde hair. She was valedictorian of our senior class and very adept physically. We were in gym class together.

Thank goodness we were in gym class together. Mrs. Kollar was our teacher. Now, Mrs. Kollar was short and wide, and she had bad eyesight. I was glad for her poor vision when she gave us our gymnastics test at the end of the year. We were spread across the whole gymnasium, and everybody had their mats out.

Mrs. Kollar said, "OK, I want you to pair up, two of you. One's an A; one's a B. I'm going to yell out what to do, then you do it."

"Barb, let's go to the back of the room." I said. "You be the A." So Barbara and I went to the back of the gymnasium.

Mrs. Kollar says, "OK, A's forward roll." Barbara gets down and does her best forward roll. "OK, B's forward roll."

"Barbara, Barbara," I said, "Be a B, be a B and do a forward roll for me." Barbara did a forward roll and I stood there out of breath!

"OK, A's backward roll." Barbara did her backward roll. "B's backward roll."

"Barbara, Barbara do a backward roll, do a backward roll." She did another one. So Barbara did everything twice as I stood there looking exhausted, saying, "Oh, gosh, oh, *phew. This is really hard work." That's how I got through and passed gym class in high school.*

Barbara and I went on to the same college together. Our college had an exchange program in California where Barbara and I attended during our junior year. We drove cross country in 1970, two women taking ten days to drive from New Jersey to California. It was fabulous. We had a great time. We went through college together, and then something happened in our senior year. I can't tell you exactly what because I don't remember. We had a falling out, and lost touch with each other. That was that until twenty-two years later.

When my dad died, I put his obituary in the hometown newspaper back in New Jersey. Barbara's mother saw it and let Barbara know about it. Barbara sent me a sympathy card remembering good things about my Dad. She reminisced about the time my parents, who owned a candy store, went on vacation and Barbara and I watched the store for a week. Next she wrote, "Would you like to correspond? Would you like to keep in touch?" And I thought "Yeah, that would be great."

So I sat down to write a letter. How do I write a letter about the last twenty-two years of my life? Alright. Well, I got married: I got divorced. I got married again: I had a kid, and I'm a chiropractor. That's twenty-two years of my life in a nutshell. And I sent the letter.

A week later I got a letter back. I opened it up, and the first thing I saw was a picture: a picture of Barbara and her cat, Gorby. I looked at her picture, and my first thought was "I ain't sending her my picture, she looks great. She looks just like she did in high school." Must have been all those forward and backward rolls that kept her in shape! I mean really she was looking good. Now to put this in perspective, I'll tell you that I teach wellness classes and I emphasize self-esteem.

I started to read the letter. The first thing Barbara said was "Isn't it wonderful that you have a son. I always wanted to have children, and I wasn't able to." And then she went on, "Isn't it wonderful that you found a profession you like, doing chiropractic and speaking. I never quite found my niche. I never quite knew what I wanted to do. I worked as a probation officer and a guidance counselor. But I never quite fit in, and I burned out. So good for you." And then she said, "I'm happily married. I married a little bit later in life, and we've been happy together for the last fifteen years," and I'm doing this, and I'm doing that." She told me about all the things she had done and the things she liked, and then she said, "And I have chronic leukemia and my prognosis was three and a half years, and I've already lived beyond that."

My mouth fell open. I took out the picture again, "I can't see it in the picture." I couldn't see it in the picture because it's not about looking good; it's about feeling good. It's about having— really having— what you do have. And I realized, all the while, I was taking for granted what I had. I have a son, isn't that great. Yes, it is great. And in that moment everything changed for me. My level of gratitude and my level of awareness changed dramatically. I suddenly realized that unless I appreciate what I have, I don't really have it. If I don't own what's mine, I cannot feel the goodness from it. I had been putting way too much of my attention on what I didn't have. I have this, but I don't have that. At the time I didn't have a husband. She's got a husband. I've got this. She's got that. You know in life we're just dealt a hand of cards. You get this; I get that. What are we going to do with what we've got? Let's accept the cards we have and not be looking over at somebody else's hand. It doesn't really matter what hand they have. This is the hand we were dealt, the only one.

Barbara and I started writing and calling on the phone. We didn't recognize each other's voices at first. That was interesting after all those hours on the phone during our high school years. And then we got together. She came to visit me, and then I went to visit her in Maryland. While I was at her house, we spent an afternoon on her screened porch. It was pouring rain, and we sat in rocking chairs under a tin roof talking about what it was like when we were teenagers, and what had happened when we separated and about the events in our lives. We just rocked the afternoon away and had a wonderful time making plans to go back to New Jersey, to her parent's home. The same home they had lived in for the last fifty-five years. The home where I'd spent many days and nights. And we planned on having a big reunion. We were going to have a really healthy weekend visiting all the places where we hung out in high school--the Dairy Queen, Federici's Pizzeria, and McDonald's. OK, we weren't exactly going to have a low-fat weekend.

But Barbara died before we could have our reunion. I decided to follow through with my plans anyway, and I went to visit Barbara's mother. I stayed at the same home, in the same room, where Barbara had lived. Her mother and I spent the weekend reminiscing about all the times we'd spent together so many years ago. Her mother gave me Barbara's old charm bracelet that weekend. Each charm represented something significant from her younger life that Barbara wanted to remember. Seeing her charms reminded me of the many things she cherished.

When we sat on the porch that day I asked her, "Barbara how you do it? How do you do it? How do you get the courage? How do you face what you're facing?"

She said, "I just do it. I do what I need to do. I've made some changes in order to improve the quality of my life for whatever time I have left." She continued, "So that's why I live in this house now." She told me her story: "We lived in a little townhouse, and I had a little plot of land, and you know I'm a gardener. I love to garden. Remember my mother was a gardener?" (Oh, I remembered her mother's gardens: they were gorgeous.) "I wanted that. So my parents gave me my inheritance early so I could buy a house and have my English Garden in the front, and my vegetables on the side, and my flower garden over here, and my hummingbird garden over there."

Visiting her house was like taking a wonderful tour. Enjoying her home lengthened her life, not only in time, but especially in quality. She made lots of changes in her exercise and nutrition and in appreciating what she had for the time she had it. For Barbara it was all about courage. And it is for you, too

There are two fatal errors that keep
great projects from coming to life:
1. Not finishing
2. Not starting

Buddha

Chapter 7
The Game Plan

Making a plan is turning knowledge into action. Making a plan is like writing the recipe you will use to bake a cake. You need the recipe to assemble the ingredients and transform them into the final product—the cake. And you need to have *all* the ingredients available. The work you did with the health triangle is analogous to getting the kitchen ready. It's easier to bake a cake if you have everything you need, if you know exactly where to find it, and if the kitchen is spotless. Now that the kitchen *is* ready, let's talk about making *your* recipe.

All plans (baking a cake, taking a trip, or reaching your own significant goal) need the following seven steps to make them usable and effective:

1. **To make it real, write it down.**

   There's something about getting it outside your gray matter and onto a piece of paper or computer screen that gives your plan a life of its own. It's no longer just a fleeting thought or a random idea. It's defined; it's been separated from the rest and crowned "Queen for the Day"!

Okay, go get a piece of paper and a pencil. Now here's where you start writing your steps. C'mon, now is all there is, remember? A journey of a thousand miles starts with a piece a paper and a pencil!

2. State your goal using all the following guidelines:

 a. It should be simple and brief.

 b. Use all positive words.

 c. Use your perspective (use "I" or "my").

 d. Achievement of the goal is measurable.

 e. It is attainable within 30-90 days.

Example: I will bake and decorate a three-tiered wedding cake by September 10.

3. Start with the big picture and then fill in the details.

You start with the finished product and work backward to see the parts. Start with the cake. The finished product is a white three-tiered wedding cake with strawberry filling, coconut frosting with real yellow daisies, and four-inch bride and groom figures on the top. After we visualize the cake, we look at each individual element: the filling, the icing, the flowers, and the couple. Then take each

90

element and look at the ingredients, the tools, the skills, the recipe, and anything else we need to create that part of our masterpiece.

4.   **Put everything into a logical sequence.**
     Develop each part in sequence and then put all the steps into sequence. Decide if some smaller sequences can be done at the same time, for example, mixing the frosting while the cake is baking. Ask if certain steps need to be complete before others are started. Estimate the time required to finish each step and each sequence. Now you're starting to see a step-by-step plan to create your fabulous wedding cake.

After you've written this first rough draft, use the next two steps to revise, refine and work out the kinks.

5.   **Ask the following questions about your project:**
     a.   Is it *possible* for you to do? Maybe not today because you don't have everything you need, but is it possible to do? Where will you need help?

b. Do you think you *can do* it? Again, not this minute but given the right ingredients, some coaching, etc. Do you think you can do this? Where do you need more knowledge or support?

c. Is it something you *want* to do? In other words, you're doing it because you want to, not because someone talked you into it or you think you should do it.

6. Read your entire plan aloud to hear how it sounds.

If something doesn't sound right go back and make sure your goal is possible, achievable, and acceptable. Now check to see if your plan includes all essential elements: time, money, materials, knowledge, skills, workspace and support. Look again for areas where other corrections may be needed.

When your plan looks similar to the sample on the next page (level of detail and completion dates) you are ready to move on to the last step...

7. **State it, date it, sign it, and breathe.**

Use your imagination and creativity to make a poster or write a statement defining your final result on parchment or other special paper and sign it, frame it and put it where you will see it everyday. This is an agreement with yourself to do what you want to do. This is your goal. Just what you wanted: your prize, your gift, your new life. Now breathe.

Sample Plan

Here's a sample plan written by my good friend Monique. After ten years in marketing, she decided it was time to go after the position held by her boss, with another company. She wrote the following plan after reading the book and following the steps in this chapter:

Goal: I have the new job I want by March 15th

The Big Picture:

1. Self-care

    a. Physical
    b. Emotional
    c. Mental

2. Define "ideal" job.

3. Research jobs and companies.

4. Write a resumé.

5. Find prospective employers.

6. Apply.

7. Interview.

8. Receive offers.

9. Negotiate.

10. Accept job.

11. Celebrate.

Detailed steps arranged in sequence:

1. Self-care: Modify behavior by implementing answers discovered in each area:
   a. Physical: Turn computer off by 9:00 P.M. to *get more sleep*.
   b. Emotional: Negotiate realistic deadlines to *lower stress level* at work.
   c. Mental: Eat regularly to prevent low blood sugar that causes *unclear thinking*.
   d. Identify support system. Ask for help with my plan!

Start: Now   **Complete: Ongoing**

2. Define ideal job:
   a. Relocate or stay in local area?
   b. Corporate, association, non-profit?
   c. Salary?
   d. Length of commute?
   e. Level of responsibility?

Start: Now   **Complete: August 25th**

3. Research:
   a. Look for search engines to be used.
   b. Search the internet for industry trends.
   c. Search the internet for industry trends in salary.

Start: Now   **Complete: August 20th**

4. Write resume:
   a. Catalog industry specific work experiences.
   b. Create resumé format.
   c. Find resumé advisor if needed.
   d. Create an alternative resumé that is recruiter-friendly

Start: August 15th   **Complete: September 15th**

5. Find prospective employers:
    a. List with three online search engines.
    b. Sign up with three recruiters.
    c. Network, network, network!

Start: September 15th   Complete: September 30th

6. Apply:
    a. Set up for at least one appointment per week.
    b. Research companies again.
    c. Revise resumé.
    d. Buy new suit for interviews.

Start: September 22nd   Complete: Ongoing

7. Interview:
    a. Prepare for interview: know the job description, review the business and the company, make list of questions to ask during interview.
    b. Get plenty of rest the night before.
    c. Send thank you note following each interview.

Ongoing: Prepare a few days before each interview

8. Receive offers:
    a. Stay optimistic and positive!
    b. Don't accept immediately--take a few days to think everything through.

Ongoing

9. Negotiate:
    a. State minimum salary both wanted and needed
    b. Be prepared to ask for additional item as to what I want and need
10. Accept job: take the new job.

Start: Now   Complete: March 15

11. CELEBRATE FOR AS LONG AS YOU LIKE!

Try? There is no try.
There is only do or do not do.

Yoda, "The Empire Strikes Back"

Chapter 8
Stay the Course

You've worked hard to complete your plan. Enjoy it with a brief celebration. Now, let's get moving again. Without a commitment there is no power:

> *Until one is committed,*
> *there is hesitancy, the chance to draw back,*
> *always ineffectiveness.*
> *Concerning all acts of initiative (and creation)*
> *there is one elementary truth,*
> *the ignorance of which kills countless ideas*
> *and splendid plans:*
> *that the moment one definitely commits oneself,*
> *then Providence moves too.*
> *All sorts of things occur to help one*
> *that would never otherwise have occurred.*
> *A whole stream of events issues from the decision,*
> *raising in one's favour all manner*
> *of unforeseen incidents and meetings*
> *and material assistance*
> *which no man [or woman] could have dreamt*
> *would have come his [or her] way.*
>
> *Whatever you can do or dream you can, begin it.*
> *Boldness has genius, power, and magic in it.*
> *Begin it Now.*
> *-Goethe*

Start today. Did you get that part? Start. Today. Start today. "Begin it Now." I know there are exceptional things going on in your life today that make starting difficult. The baby isn't feeling well. You have company coming for dinner. Your husband's birthday is tomorrow. The washing machine just broke. You've got a report due at work. So? That's your life, right? Do you think the Red Sea is going to part when you are ready to start? Neither do I. I didn't say complete it today. I didn't say do a lot today. I said, "START." It could be jotting down a short list of reminders you need for the next step. Something like "Shopping list: buy pans, rolling pin, icing, and wedding couple at the restaurant supply store." Just make the list. We are breaking this down into small steps, so you can do one at a time. You've made your map. You are in the car now, and you are covering one mile at a time.

Ask for help. No woman is an island. You cannot do this alone. Look, I am the original Lone Ranger. I did everything on my own, by myself. My script was, "I can do it by myself, thank you very much. No, I don't need any help, thanks again. I'll just do it by myself. No, really, it's no trouble. I *always* do it by myself." Phew! I get exhausted just reading the past few lines.

So one of the glitches that will stop you every time is refusing to ask for help (or being unable or unwilling to ask). Poor Tonto. He wanted to help. He was ready to help. He had so little to do. All he wanted was to make the Lone Ranger's life easier and all the Lone Ranger could say was, "No, I do it alone, Tonto."

Ask yourself, "How do I feel when someone I love or admire asks me for help?" If you answered, "I'd want to help them," that was the answer I was looking for. (If you said you didn't want to, then you're burned out and need a vacation!) It feels good to help those we care about. And it follows that it feels good for others to help you. There is no double standard here, although many of you have set one up. So ask for the help you need. And don't let a "no" from someone who knows how to say it without guilt stop you from asking the next person.

Keep your eyes on the destination. Focus on the outcome you have committed to. It's easy to switch your focus to the everyday tasks and obstacles demanding your attention. Imagine you are driving along the highway, and you get a flat

101

tire. You can stand there for the rest of the day looking at the flat tire, yelling at the flat tire, kicking the flat tire or ignoring the flat tire. None of that is going to change the flat tire. You either need to call someone to change the tire, or you need to change it yourself. Only when it's fixed can you get back in the car and go on your merry way. It's the same with your goal. When obstacles arise, deal with them, accept them and move on. Keep your plan within reach, within your vision.

Take action every day. Reread your plan often. It's *your* game plan. You might forget where you are going or how to get there without two actions: reviewing your plan regularly and doing at least one thing, anything, something, no matter how small it might appear, every single day.

Set short term goals within the larger one. When I used to look at my appointment book for the week, I was overwhelmed with all the meetings and scheduled appointments because it felt like I would be doing everything all at once. I was seeing them simultaneously, all on one page, and feeling like I would be doing everything at one time, too. I started to tell myself I was going to keep each appointment, one at a time. One person at a time. As long as I kept my focus on the present moment and the present task, I was never overwhelmed. One thing at a time, one step at a time, one after another, that's all any of us can do. Then it feels just right.

Celebrate your progress everyday.
Acknowledgement is where you do a self-assessment without judgment. Example: "I said I would exercise three times this week for thirty minutes. I exercised two times for thirty minutes." I just acknowledge what I did. It's a fact. There's no emotion, judgment, critical evaluation, or excuse.

What not to say: "I know that I said I was going to exercise three times, but Sandy had a party one day, and I couldn't get out the other day because it rained. I know I should have done three times anyway, but I always try to do too much, and then this happens. I just feel horrible about it all." PLEASE, STOP IT! You either did it or you didn't. It's okay. It's done. Move on!

Acknowledge the completion of each short term goal as you reach it. Celebrate in some way that feels good to you. Buy yourself flowers. Read a new book. Get a manicure. Have lunch with a good friend at your favorite restaurant. Something that says, "Good job, you are doing it, keep going."

Rewards will be different for everyone and will be different for you at different times. Stop and listen to yourself and figure out what would be a wonderful present for a job well-done. Reward your action with more enjoyable action.

Recognize a detour is not a dead end. Whoa, Nellie. Yes, you heard that right. When you are driving and encounter a detour, do you stop there, get out of the car, and walk away? Of course you don't. You have to slow down, maybe stop, and think about how you are going to proceed *differently*. What you were planning will no longer work. Period. So what is the alternate route? Usually there is an alternate route mapped out for you. It may be inconvenient. It may take a few minutes longer, but it will get you where you're going. Isn't that what you wanted all along?

When you meet with delays and detours realize you will have to change, amend or add to your plan given the reality of things and the present state of your world. Some things are outside of your control, so you must adapt.

Even without a detour to challenge you, it's a good idea to think about what you can add to your original plan. Have you had new insights since you began? Probably. Have your circumstances changed so that you need more or fewer (if you can count them) steps now? What changes have taken place in your life situation to make it better? Or could you do things differently? If you get a bonus at work, you might be able to speed things up. If a loved one dies, you will probably want to take time off. These are changes, delays, alterations. They are not "I quits." They are not places to stop. They are not places to give up.

Learn from the obstacles and challenges you encounter as you move toward your goal. Notice where you get a little shaky and maybe ready to jump ship. Pay attention. Here's where you run the risk that silly amnesia will come in to get you off track for a day, a month, a lifetime! This is where the learning comes in. Here's where you learn more about who you are and what does and doesn't work well for you. You are gathering information on how YOU reach your goals and what gets in YOUR way. Watch for yellow flags and deal with them before they turn into red ones!

Adopt an attitude of play. Make your journey a game. It is anyway. All of life is a game. There are other players and rules, guidelines and strategies, getting to the end of the board with or without money, and other stuff! Remember, "It's not

whether you win or lose, its how you play (enjoy) the game."
Yes, of course you want to win. But it feels terrible to be a sore
loser and even worse to be a sore winner! Pretend you are a
five-year-old child for a moment, and you will automatically
see life becomes a game!

When my son Micah was ten years old, washing the dishes
was one of his regular chores. Sometimes he would face away
from the sink with his arms behind his back while washing the
dishes. I'd say, "Micah, don't play around. Just wash the
dishes." What I was really saying was, "Do it the way I do it,
the same every time. The plates go here, the glasses go here,
and don't have any fun. Turn it into hard work. Make it
boring. Make it something to dread." He made it play, fun and
a game. Good for him. He taught me well and years later I
appreciated his teachings!

Persistence is everything. The best definition of
persistence is enduring continuance. You continue one step at
a time, one pound at a time, one dollar at a time, one minute at
a time, one word at a time with whatever goal you are moving
toward. Patience is helpful, to put it mildly. That's an
understatement. Patience is defined as:

1. The will or ability to wait or endure without complaint, or
2. Steadiness, endurance, or perseverance in the performance of a task.

If you don't have patience when you start, your journey is a great opportunity to learn it.

Flexibility is useful and essential. You will need to change or adapt your plans as you proceed. When you finally get rolling, the last thing you want to do is change. But we have already anticipated changes in the plan, so it will be easier to adapt to unforeseen circumstances. Remember, we talked about change earlier and how change was the only thing in life you could really count on? This is no different. As you and the circumstances change, your flexibility will help insure success. Because of change, new possibilities that affect the whole process may come into play suggesting new and better outcomes that might far exceed your original goal. Check in regularly with your triangle, your personal balance system. Which side could use some reinforcement? Which side has too much interference?

Attain workability, then perfectibility. Trying to make things perfect will keep you from trying at all (or exhaust you and cause you to quit in frustration). I learned about writing a book from Gerry Robert, a tremendous marketing executive and motivational speaker. He says, "Get it down, *then* get it right." I use the same approach with dancing. When the music plays, I want to get out on the floor and enjoy myself dancing with my partner. First, I have to learn the rhythm. Then the steps. Then practice the technique. Then learn more steps with more technique. Then work the steps into routines. And with each layer my dancing gains depth and style and pizzazz. It starts with workability and improves from there.

You now have the tools you need to stay the course for as long as it takes to reach your goal. By keeping these reminders in front of you, you'll be able to find just the right helpful hint for each occasion. And before you know it you're at the finish line, getting what you've always wanted and feeling great!

It is good to have an end
to journey toward;
but it is the journey that
matters in the end.

Ursula K. LeGuin

Chapter 9
Crossing the Finish Line!

Have you ever stopped to think about your life five or ten or even fifteen years ago and exclaimed, "I would have never imagined I'd be here today, doing this job, living in this place with this person."

Sometimes I joke around calling myself a "Dancing Fool." What with dance lessons every week for over four years and scheduling big band dance weekends throughout the year, not to mention a wardrobe full of long, flowing skirts and dresses.

You remember my favorite story, the one about meeting with a life coach? That was the start of my life as it is today. I asked questions and found answers and then followed up with lots of action. I listened to quiet thoughts and found ways to follow through as if on a treasure hunt.

Where would I be if I hadn't taken action on each one of those positive thoughts? What if I hadn't recognized or even been aware action was necessary and essential if I was to change my life totally? I could be going through each day keeping myself busy. I would be doing things I enjoyed with lots of friends yet still pretending I didn't really want what I have today.

Maybe you're in that place now, pretending. Maybe while you read this book it sounds pretty good or maybe it sounds really, really fabulous. Maybe you are at an important fork in the road, and you recognize you have new choices to make. Which way will you go, the same tired road or one that's completely new?

If you've taken the time and energy so far to decide what you want, where you've come from so far, where you want to go, and what you need to get there, then good for you. No, *really*, good for you! That's an accomplishment all in itself.

But here's a secret I haven't shared. You know how you need to start at point A then move to point B and follow the plan step-by-step to get where you want? What you don't know, can't know beforehand, is what's going to happen along the way. Who are you going to meet? What are you actually going to do? What wonderful new ideas are going to come to light? What will you learn about yourself? What will you learn about *your* life? What will you learn about life itself?

I used to fantasize that I would meet the man of my dreams in some romantic way. Like a Meg Ryan/Tom Hanks movie—

take your pick which one! Really, I held onto this romantic notion for about fifteen years. On second thought, I may have had this notion from the time I heard about Cinderella and Prince Charming! I just knew it would happen in a way where I didn't have to do anything. I could just wait for him to show up. It took at least fifteen years to realize, "Hmmm, this isn't working. Maybe I need to do something else."

Why do I tell you this? Because maybe you will see some of yourself in me and say, "What I've been doing hasn't gotten me what I want. I keep going through the same maze and expecting to find a piece of cheese at the end of it. I haven't found it yet. Oh well, there's always tomorrow." Remember, all there is, is NOW.

Imagine how you want your life to be and...

1. Look honestly at your strengths and the areas that need reinforcement.
2. Decide how you want your life to be.
3. Prepare your plan.
4. Commit yourself.
5. Do something (anything) that starts you toward your goal.
6. Trust yourself.
7. Love yourself.
8. Stick with it
9. Get help when you need it.
10. Follow your plan and win the prize.

YES, IT *IS* ALL ABOUT YOU

When you cross the finish line CELEBRATE! Do it immediately. Give yourself some well-earned, delayed gratification. Reinforce the behavior that got you to the completion of your plan and the achievement of a significant life goal. Let yourself feel successful.

Act successful. Etch this feeling in your mind with an appropriate ceremony or prize to provide tangible proof of your accomplishment. After a race there is an award or a trophy. Do whatever provides you recognition. Have a party with all the people who helped along the way. Enjoy a weekend away at a spa. Buy a new outfit complete with shoes and purse to match. Choose something that signifies you have what it takes, you did what you had to, and you reached your goal through planning, persistence, flexibility, and commitment. Say congratulations to yourself. Treat yourself the way you would treat your best friend if she had just achieved the same goal. Hmmm.

Take time out. Take a bow. Take a break. Take a nap. Take a deep breath. Now, what's your next goal? Write it here!

Life is pretty simple: You do some stuff. Most fails. Some works. You do more of what works. If it works big, others quickly copy it. Then you do something else. The trick is the doing something else.

Leonardo daVinci

The Doctor *is* In

Dr. Eisenberg is available to answer your questions and help guide you through using this book to your best advantage. Call for a personal consultation to find out how.

For more information contact:

Jenna Eisenberg, D.C.

0N730 Pleasant Hill Road

Wheaton, Illinois 60187

630-653-4195

jenna.eisenberg@comcast.net

Speaking Engagements

Jenna Eisenberg is available for speaking engagements at conferences and meetings. For more information, please contact:

Email: Jenna.Eisenberg@comcast.net
Web: www.JennaEisenberg.com

Write to

Jenna Eisenberg

I hope this book has changed your life. I would like to hear from you. Please write to me and let me know how this book has made a difference.

Send letter or email to

Jenna Eisenberg
0N730 Pleasant Hill Road
Wheaton, Illinois 60187

Email: Jenna.Eisenberg@comcast.net

ABOUT THE AUTHOR

For over thirty years Dr. Jenna Eisenberg has been motivating people to take care of themselves <u>and</u> have fun in the process!

Jenna grew up in Englishtown, a small town in New Jersey. She and her family lived above the candy store. As a child, she worked alongside her parents and entertained the customers with a song, a dance, or a story or two.

She now lives in the Chicago suburbs with Ed, the man of her dreams. They can be found any weekend out on the dance floor doing the foxtrot, the jitterbug or the rumba!